VOICES UNDERFOOT

MEMORY, FORGETTING, AND ORAL VERBAL ART

ANGELA BOURKE

This essay is part of the interdisciplinary series *Famine Folios*, covering many aspects of the Great Hunger in Ireland from 1845–52.

CONTENTS

Figure 1 | Daniel Macdonald, *Sidhe Gaoithe/The Fairy Blast* [Detail]

INTRODUCTION

The dead stand at ease in Pádraic Reaney's *The Last Visit 1* at Ireland's Great Hunger Museum, their bony authority contrasting with the pale and silent figures of the Famine emigrants above them **[Cover]**. Born in 1952, Reaney was brought up speaking Irish in Connemara, County Galway, not far from the home of celebrated writer Máirtín Ó Cadhain, in whose satirical novel *Cré na Cille* the characters are all dead, entertaining themselves in the graveyard with the same disputes and spiteful backbiting they carried on in life.

Reaney's work reminds us of the tender care that people in the west of Ireland still give their dead, laying them in consecrated ground among ancestors and neighbors, often by the sea. Some communities line graves with flowers or green moss; others carefully cover a coffin with straw before allowing any shovelful of earth or sand to fall on it; mourners stay to witness the filling of the grave and the last, reverent tucking in of the deceased. Graves endure as sites of human connection, but, a century after the Famine, fields and roadsides where victims fell and were hastily interred continued to prompt anger and distress, and some people could still relate the names and intimate details of people dead from hunger. This essay is an attempt to trace lines of memory and forgetting through oral history and verbal art, from the physical experience of Famine in the 1840s to the visual art of our own time, examining one man's stories about fairies as a vernacular magical realism that attempted to get to grips with what could not be forgotten.

A SOCIETY IN TENSION:
SÍDHE GAOITHE/THE FAIRY BLAST (1842)

Cork artist Daniel Macdonald exhibited *Sídhe Gaoithe/The Fairy Blast* **[Figure 1]** at the Cork Art Union in 1842, when he was twenty-two (O'Sullivan, *Lion's Den* 37–44). Something terrifying lies ahead of his large party caught in sudden wind under a dark sky: horses and riders are wide-eyed with fear, as is the bareheaded, barefoot young woman facing us. With eight others, she walks ahead of a laden cart that emerges between walls of rock, with two more faces just visible behind it. The driver leads his horse through eddying dust while the woman seated atop his load covers her mouth. On her right, the rider in the tall hat looks like a gentleman, perhaps a landlord, as he urges his horse forward with cape flying, his pipe clenched between his teeth. The cautious horseman on the viewer's right, whose red-kerchiefed wife rides pillion behind him, is probably a well-off farmer, sporting leather saddle, boots, and stirrups.

The people on foot represent the burgeoning rural class of poor, Irish-speaking, small farmers and laborers. Women clutch cloaks and shawls around them, and only one or two of them wear shoes. They look well fed, their clothes clean and colorful enough to appeal to art buyers in the city, but within a few years most of them will be reduced to rags and destitution.

When Macdonald painted this scene, the stage was already set for the catastrophe that would overwhelm Ireland. The country's population had risen steeply after about 1760, as the potato became a subsistence crop, and the 1841 census figure of 8,175,000 – almost a third of the United Kingdom's total – included at least three million who ate little else. By 1845, when blight struck, Ciarán Ó Murchadha suggests, "little ... was left of the solidarity some historians have seen as linking landlord and community in a nexus of mutual respect and co-operation in the late eighteenth century" (11, 17; cf. Whelan 87–9).

This painting's title derives from oral traditions about fairies. *Sí-ghaoth* – a fairy wind, or "blast" (sometimes anglicized "shee-gwee") – reflects a widespread belief that sudden gusts occur when the so-called "good people" move through the air, causing damage as they go.[1] During Macdonald's childhood in Cork, his father's friend

Figure 1 | Daniel Macdonald, *Sídhe Gaoithe/The Fairy Blast*

9

Thomas Crofton Croker, by then based in London, had published *Fairy Legends and Traditions of the South of Ireland* to great acclaim.[2] Jacob and Wilhelm Grimm's fairy tales had appeared in Germany in 1812, but Croker's was the first collection of oral tales from the UK. Irish fairy legends tell of people swept away, like W. B. Yeats's "The Stolen Child" (1886), and replaced with withered, cantankerous changelings, and describe crops "blasted" by salt winds or disease. After 1845, "blast" meant the deadly new fungus *Phytophthora infestans*.

Fairies in these legends live in the air and the sea and under certain hills, usually invisible and unheard. They can impinge capriciously on humans, however, especially during transitions and upheavals, and so represent the immanent unknown: uncertainty, ambivalence, and human powerlessness. The people most at risk from fairies are young women and male children, like the figures lit most brightly in the painting, and twilight is the most dangerous time.[3] Milk may sour, fruit may rot, and people or animals may suddenly fall ill by their agency, but the most likely places to encounter the fairies are far from domestic activity, on boundaries and borderlands, like Macdonald's mountain pass. While his landscape looks more Italian than Irish, the gnarled tree he shows growing from the cliff suggests a "lone bush", or fairy thorn, which should never be disturbed.

The cart and the riders have traveled a distance, perhaps from a market town on the other side of the mountain, but the people on foot carry nothing, and seem to have come uphill from the viewer's side to meet them; the barrel and boxes on the cart could be destined for a wedding or a wake. The painting's title indicates the supernatural dangers that would have been part of their consciousness, complicating the hazards of a mountain road in changing weather.

Painting this large and diverse group in such a setting, Macdonald combines vernacular verbal art with ideas of the sublime and the Gothic to represent a society in tension, divided by language and culture. Mostly barefoot and female, arguably also impulsive and improvident, because shown empty-handed, the poorest people here have placed themselves almost under the horses' hooves. The leading woman's bare legs and head emphasize her vulnerability and sexuality, but she and her people endanger their more prosperous neighbors and impede the progress of the virile landlord figure the artist has made central – the only one who shows no fear. Daniel Macdonald's painting anticipates the rhetoric of the Famine, and hints at how it came to be remembered and forgotten.

MEMORY AND FORGETTING:
THE ELEPHANT IN THE LANDSCAPE

In 1995, when the time came to commemorate the Great Famine, it had scarcely been spoken of in Ireland for twenty-five years. Code for anti-English bitterness since the Land War of the early 1880s, the Northern Ireland Troubles had made it rhetorically redundant among nationalists, and taboo for so-called revisionists.[4] Parliamentary exchanges about Famine-commemoration plans make clear that it was a potential minefield, with government determined to defuse tension and avert embarrassment by emphasizing academic research and humanitarian aid over local memory.[5]

Famine stories are commoner in North America, where millions claim ancestors who used their last resources to pay their passage or were "emigrated" at the expense of landlords or benevolent societies. Robert Scally notes that Famine emigrants to North America took so little with them across the ocean that the "great majority ... were in effect stripped of their outward diversity and reduced to the axioms of their culture". Irish American identity emerged, he suggests, from the trauma of leaving Ireland: "Most actually saw the land of their nativity fading into the sea as they sailed westward. For the Famine emigrants, it was a revelation unimaginable just weeks before, sudden and experienced by masses of them simultaneously, shipload after shipload, year after year (230–6; cf. Brighton).

While Irish Americans were building community on memories of hunger, people in Ireland were busy forgetting, for reasons of shame and stigma, and perhaps, as Cormac Ó Gráda suggests, because the worst affected were too traumatized to speak or because nobody wanted to listen (*Black '47* 210–12, "Famine" 130–5). He emphasizes the propensity of famine to divide societies and destroy cultural systems ("Famine" 129, 141), pointing out the violently unbalanced effect such catastrophes have on those already poor, and finding that the "collective or communal memory" that the 1995–97 commemorations often invoked was "in large part artifact or myth" ("Famine" 122). How, then, did people in Ireland go about forgetting, and what kind of memories remained?

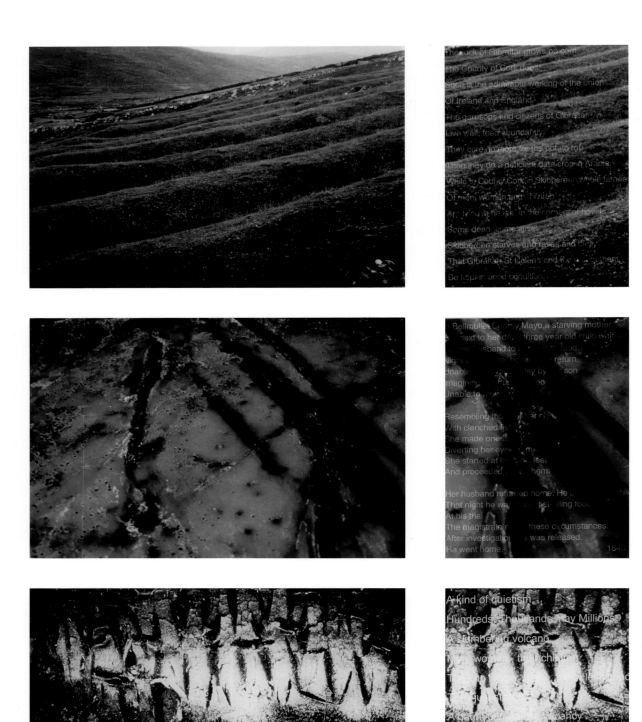

Figure 2 | Alanna O'Kelly, *A Kind of Quietism*

DAVID THOMSON, *WOODBROOK*, AND POTATOES

A celebrated memoir of the last days of landlordism gives a sense of the enduring divisions famine brought to one Irish estate. In the 1930s David Thomson, a student of modern history and later a writer and BBC radio producer, spent his Oxford vacations at a landlord's house in County Roscommon. He was eighteen when he became tutor to the Kirkwood family's two daughters, and sixty-one in 1974 when he published *Woodbrook*, naming his book after the house, and weaving lyrical, sometimes disturbing, personal memories among what he had learned, on the ground and in libraries, about the Famine.

Woodbrook appeared five years into the Troubles, when Irish history was hotly contested, but the ideas that led to the Field Day Theatre Company's beginnings in 1980 were already incubating. Its co-founder, playwright Brian Friel, became Thomson's friend and promoter, as did poet Seamus Heaney. They saw immediately, as Heaney wrote in 2001, that the book was not just a love story but a "work of historical reconstruction ... [that] contrived also to tell the story of other realities – social, cultural, historical and political – that had been central to Irish life for centuries" (*Guardian*, February 21, 2001).

The nearest town to Woodbrook was Carrick-on-Shannon, where the derelict workhouse, built in 1841 to accommodate eight hundred paupers, still housed the offices of Leitrim County Council. Thomson was fascinated by how little anyone said about the building's past:

The only reminder of its workhouse days lies covered in dust on the floor of an upstairs room of a block to the left of the main entrance where the Board of Guardians held their meetings in the years succeeding the Irish Poor Law of 1838 – I mean the large piles of huge leather-bound volumes of their minutes written in various hands (156–7).

The Irish Poor Law of 1838 required landowners to pay a "poor rate" for the relief of poverty in their districts, and provided for the building of workhouses. "Guardians" elected from among the landowners administered the system in each area, but many were already in debt and resorted to mass evictions when the Famine took hold. In the words of a contemporary observer, the "system intended to relieve the poor, by making the landlords responsible for their welfare, has at once made it the interest, and therefore the duty, of the landlords to get rid of them" (*Illustrated London News* (*ILN*), December 22, 1849).

David Thomson spent days in the old workhouse – now an impressive visitor attraction – reading the huge minute books. Rejected for military service because of poor eyesight, he returned to Woodbrook in 1939 when war broke out, to labor full-time on its farm, developing an intimate sense of landlord–tenant relations and of the persistence of certain memories. Walking through the pastures on his first day there in 1932, he had noticed markings on the ground like the ridges Alanna O'Kelly chose almost sixty years later for the top panels of *A Kind of Quietism*, her photomontage with text at Ireland's Great Hunger Museum **[Figure 2]**:

I observed many low curved undulations of the turf, straight and regularly spaced, the valleys between them three feet apart, the ridges sloping upwards with the hill, never across it, all obviously made by men, but it did not occur to me for years that they were potato beds abandoned with their rotten crop by the starving people who fled or died in the Great Famine, eighty-five years before. And when I met the Maxwell brothers, who lived with their parents on Woodbrook farm and worked there, I did not know that they were the great-great-grandchildren of the only survivors in that townland, nor that their little house had been one of thirty at that time, each standing in its own plot of several acres, every one of which had been pulled down in the years of the famine, nor that they felt ashamed because they knew why their house had been spared, nor that they secretly cherished hatred for the Major, their present landlord and employer, whom in day to day relationships they loved – cherished this hatred because of his ancestors and theirs, and because it might help in their advancement (10).

Thomson calls Tommy and Jimmy Maxwell "great-great-grandchildren" of Famine survivors, but the connection was much closer: their grandparents had been the survivors, and their parents, Michael and Nanny, were able to give him first-hand information.

Nanny Maxwell, born at Woodbrook in the 1860s, told Thomson that some of her fourteen older siblings had starved to death on the estate. Her parents often talked about "the hunger and the fever and the terrible evictions", she said, but her brothers always walked out the door, saying "Don't be telling us about those bad times" (56, 173, 175). In 1848 Major Kirkwood's ancestor had persuaded her father to help evict the other tenants, including some of his relatives who died soon after, in return for his own family's continued tenure (177–8). When debt eventually forced the Kirkwoods to sell, the Maxwell brothers led a boycott of their auction, and bought Woodbrook themselves after the war (Thomson 303–4, 321; Vignoles 134–5).

Potatoes were an inescapable link with "those bad times", and Thomson indicates the memory and emotion they could elicit:

Once, at the fair of Boyle when I was buying seed potatoes with Tommy Maxwell's expert help, I saw on an ass-cart a small load of a variety I had never seen before, white ones with bluish-red markings. I wanted to try them. He said no one would buy them and that it was a poor mountainy man that was selling them who would drive his ass home in the evening with the load on the cart the same as he drove in to town. The potatoes were "Blacksmith's" he said, the kind that everybody grew in the "bad times" – the famine times. I persuaded him to let me buy a few, enough for a couple of ridges, but he was very upset. We planted them at the side of the field. They got the blight. The rest of our crop – about six acres – grew perfectly (173).

The best-remembered potato variety grown in Famine times was the coarse, heavy-cropping Lumper, but two generations later Tommy Maxwell recognized Blacksmiths by eye and remembered them by name. He was right to resist buying them: growing blight-susceptible potato varieties beside resistant ones could create an infection pressure for the main crop, and the stigmatized variety in this case was probably heavily infected by viruses.[6]

In the 1930s, on horseback or cycling with the Kirkwood daughters, David Thomson often looked for, but never found, a mysterious "Stirabout Road" near Woodbrook, built during the Famine by hungry laborers who each received a bowl of porridge, or stirabout, for their work (17). He got to know field names such as "Flanagan's Rock" and "Martin's Garden" as he might have learned the names of streets in a town – without curiosity – until Nanny Maxwell told him about the families who had lived in the fields named after them. Although born ten years after it ended, Nanny "knew the Christian names of everyone who had lived in the townland of Usna when the famine began" (176).

Usna is now the site of Carrick-on-Shannon Golf Club: Major Kirkwood gave the land rent-free in 1944, and members raised money to buy it when the estate was sold (308). Nobody seems to have explained the name of another place that Thomson mentions often. Irish was no longer spoken in the area by his time, but most local people would probably have understood Shanwelliagh – "a rushy lowland" behind Woodbrook's stable yard, on the way to Usna – as *seanbhaile*, "the old village" (46).

SOCIAL MEMORY:
FAMINE POTS AND ORAL TESTIMONY

Most social memory of the Great Famine is intensely local, notably concrete, and has probably been reinvented and regenerated at multiple points in response to external stimuli, local contestation, or the familiar structures of oral narrative (Ó Gráda, *Black '47*, 194–225; Beiner, "Decline", *Remembering*). One recent stimulus to memory has been the Irish Famine Pots website,[7] set up in 2013 by John Cassidy and Mattie Lennon to resurrect and research the huge cast-iron soup boilers imported in their hundreds from Coalbrookedale in Shropshire following the Soup Kitchen Act of February 1847, and used outdoors to cook soup and cornmeal porridge (Kinealy, *Apparitions* 18–19) **[Figure 3]**. Cassidy and Lennon have identified more than fifty of these pots, and have

Figure 3 | Eddie "the Miller" Doherty standing in a Famine pot, Buncrana, County Donegal

been instrumental in their preservation, display, and continuing documentation. A film clip on their website tells how Cassidy's interest in these relics began in 2011 when he found a Famine pot broken in fragments near Barnesmore Gap in south Donegal. It had previously stood by the road, where local farmers heated water in it when dipping sheep. Its owner gave him permission to have it restored by welding, after which it found a new home at Leghawny Community Hall nearby.[8]

Among the contributions to the Irish Famine Pots website is a text written by a primary-school child as part of the Schools' Folklore Scheme of 1937–38, organized by the Irish Folklore Commission (IFC) in partnership with the government Department of Education (Briody 260–70) **[Figure 4]**. Based on what her father, Dan Griffin, has told her, Mary Ann Griffin of Leagans, about three miles north of Inver, County Donegal, uses the formal English of schoolroom writing to explain a local place name, the "Bracan walls". This was the scene of a fight over porridge (Irish: *brachán*) cooked in a Famine pot ninety years earlier. The porridge had been distributed, but it was spilled before anyone could eat it when opposing factions used their long-handled wooden noggins as weapons:

In the year following the potato failure, the Year of the Famine, by the Queen's orders, porridge was made in Edward Griffin's field. A big turf fire was lit and a huge pot used. Yellow meal was used and Edward Griffin the owner of the land was the Gaffer or overseer. He saw that the porridge was divided evenly. People came from Croagh, Meenawillaghan, Keelogs, Tievedooley, Drimfin, Castleogary, Parkbane and Altcor for it. They carried the porridge home in noggins. These were wooden vessels with long handles. They held about a quart of porridge. There is a crossroads beside Legan School on the Ardara and Inver road called the Bracan walls ...

In the copybook her teacher sent to the IFC in 1938, Mary Ann Griffin noted that the Edward Griffin she mentions was her father's uncle, and that "a big moss covered rock still marks the place of the fire. It is in the field beside our house and about 80 yards from Legan School".[9]

The National Folklore Collection (NFC) is kept at University College, Dublin. Among the largest such collections in the world, it is the principal source for oral testimony about the Famine, and also houses Daniel Macdonald's painting **[Figure 1]**. When the IFC was set up in 1935 with government support, on a model developed in Scandinavia, it undertook the systematic recording and archiving of local history, calendar custom, traditional beliefs and practices, and oral verbal art – chiefly stories, songs, and proverbs.[10] The website called Dúchas.ie is part of the project to digitize the NFC for open access.[11] Limited at the time of writing to material from sixteen of the twenty-six counties in the Schools' Manuscript Collection, it includes Mary Ann Griffin's pages from 1938 **[Figure 4]**.

Two books of extracts from the NFC made illuminating and harrowing contributions to the 1995–97 commemorations. Former folklore student Cathal Póirtéir produced radio series in Irish and English, and edited two compendia to accompany them (*Famine Echoes, Glórtha ón Ghorta*).[12] Accounts given in the 1930s and 1940s by children and grandchildren of people alive during the Famine convey a powerful

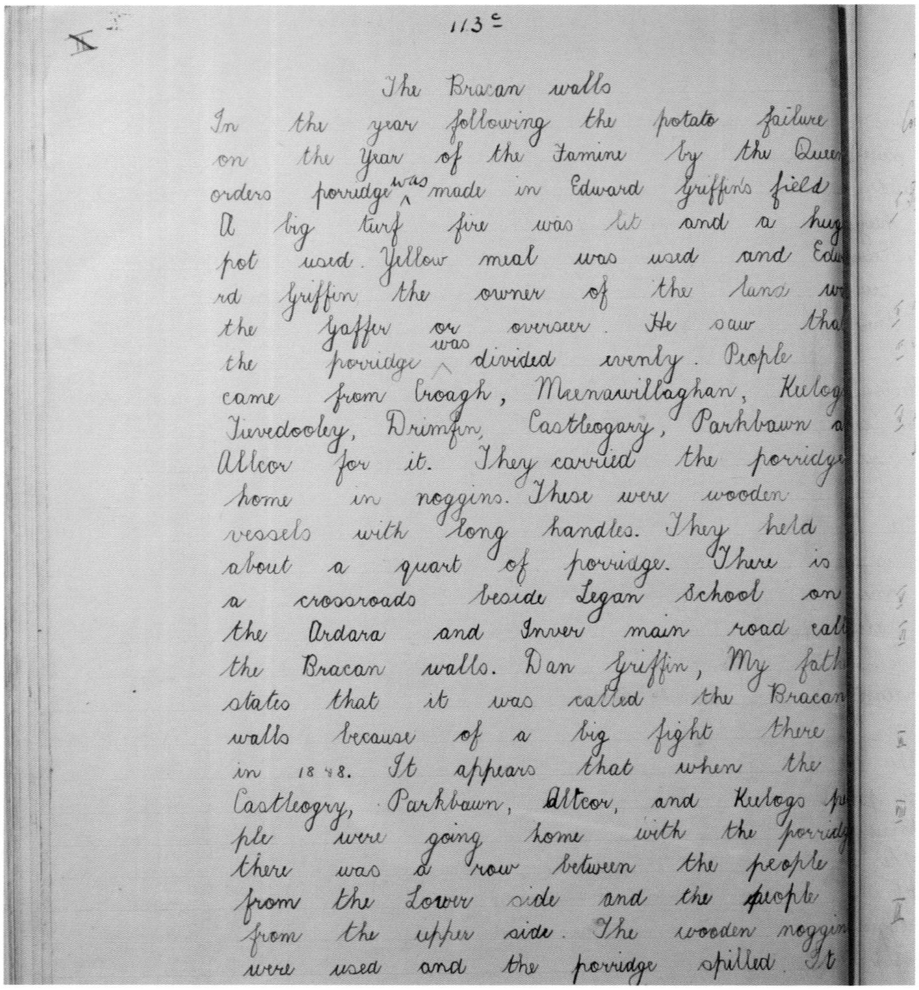

Figure 4 | Mary Ann Griffin, "The Bracan Walls"

sense of its emotional and social legacy (Póirtéir, *Famine Echoes* 13). Ned Buckley, sixty-six, of Knocknagree, County Cork, supplied extensive material in English in 1945, naming people remembered for their charity or said to have become rich at their neighbors' expense (Póirtéir, *Famine Echoes* 144, 213–14).[13] His description of improvised shelters is precise and heartbreaking:

In those days the habitations of the poor were very miserable. They lived in every kind of hovel. In a broad bounds ditch [wide, earthen boundary bank] between two farms it was usual, with [the farmer's] consent, for a poor working man to scoop the earth from the centre of the ditch leaving the shell at the sides stand in the shape of walls that could be roofed over with sticks and heath, and scraws [scraith: a sod] of tough mountain land laid down on the roofing and thatch over with rushes ... (Póirtéir, *Famine Echoes* 28).

This sort of oral history, scrupulously passed on, is part of local citizenship, bound up with known places, personal identity, and the maintenance of community. Mary

Ann Griffin showed the same care above, naming the several townlands from which people came to her granduncle's field, and mentioning the "big moss covered rock" beside her own home. Naming the links in a recognized chain of transmission vouches for the testimony's accuracy and credibility. Ned Buckley related what his eighty-four-year-old neighbor Jack Conell had told him of attempts to quarantine sick people, details Jack had learned from his father, Old Mick Conell, whom Buckley himself remembered, and "who was a full grown man" at the time of the Famine, "a labouring man":

When the people were so badly fed on greens and turnips, cabbage and certain kinds of weeds that, as they used to say, "ran down through them", they were affected with a kind of fever and dysentery that was contagious or "taking" as they used to say at that time and all the people suffering in this way were put away in a place by themselves. They built huts up against a sheltered ditch, poles were stood on the outside and a roof thrown across them to the ditch and they were thatched with brambles, briars and rushes. Here in those huts or "scalpts" the afflicted people had to live, their own people or family shunning them. There were a few of those scalpts, Jack Conell says, in the field now belonging to Willie Breen bounding the field now owned by Andrew Rahilly, Shanballa. The field or the port near the bounds ditch is a low and sheltered valley and was known as Park na Phooka. The sick poor had to have a vessel of their own and their friends would come now and again a couple of times each day and empty their own gallons containing milk or boiled potatoes or oat meal porridge into them, taking care not to touch them at all as the mere act of touching the vessels used by the sick was suppose to bring on the sickness (Póirtéir, *Famine Echoes* 106).

SCALP AT CAHUERMORE.

Figure 5 | **"Scalp at Cahuermore"**
(*Illustrated London News*, December 29, 1849)

SCALPS AND SCALPEENS
IN COUNTY CLARE

The "scalpts" of Ned Buckley's account correspond to the "scalps" of west Clare, pictured and described in the *Illustrated London News* in the winter of 1849–50 (O'Sullivan, *Tombs* 50). The recently appointed inspector of Kilrush Poor Law Union, Captain Arthur Kennedy, and a Paris-educated curate, Fr. Thomas Moloney, had drawn attention to the level of evictions in the area by landlords and their agents. Hundreds were becoming homeless every day as huge numbers of houses were demolished, and George Poulett Scrope MP had taken up their cause in Parliament (Kinealy, *Great Calamity* 287–9; Lynch 89–93). Moloney had predicted that his parish would become "another and worse Skibbereen".[14] The artist/reporter who visited west Clare for the newspaper may have been James Mahony of Cork, who had so memorably drawn and described that town in 1847 (O'Sullivan, *Tombs,* 25–30). Mahony (if it was he) sketched and described a scalp where a woman lay dying **[Figure 5]**:

On arriving at the bog of Cahuermore, I alighted at the scalp shown in the Sketch, which Mr. Monsel[15] and his companions discovered to their surprise, and found in it a woman dying of the customary fever which attends on want of food and clothing and the ordinary necessaries of life. Than this scalp, nothing could be more wretched. It was placed in a hole, surrounded by pools, and three sides of the scalp (shown in the Sketch) were dripping with water, which ran in small streams over the floor and out by the entrance. Yet, wretched as this hole is, the poor inhabitants said they would be thankful and content if the landlord would leave them there, and the Almighty would spare their lives. Its principal tenant is Margaret Vaughan ... and a more wretched history, even in this country of wretchedness, is scarcely to be found. Not far from her cave is the destroyed village of Kilmurry Strikane, another of those pictures of desolation of which I have already sent you too many (*ILN*, December 29, 1849).

Errors of transcription or typography, like the strange place names "Cahuermore" and "Kilmurry Strikane", are common in these reports. A more likely rendering of An Cheathrú Mhór, "the big quarterland", would be Carhuemore. Modern maps show it as Carrowmore, just north of Doonbeg, on the west coast of Clare. Margaret Vaughan's scalp must have been behind Doughmore beach (An Dumhach Mhór: the big sand-hill), in the reedy wetlands now dominated by the Trump International Golf Links and Hotel.

The same *ILN* report notes that in the two years to December 1849, 604 houses had been leveled in nearby "Kilmurry Strikane". That name should read Kilmurry Ibrickane, the parish where Thomas Moloney arrived as curate in 1846, aged thirty-six, and where he soon saw people dying of starvation and exposure. A ruined church and graveyard are all that remain at the crossroads, left of the road from Doonbeg to Quilty, which today's maps show simply as Kilmurry. The *ILN*'s reports and images eventually helped to feed the hungry, but its mangled versions of place names have

Figure 6 | "Scalpeen of Tim Downs, Dunmore" (*Illustrated London News*, December 22, 1849)

SCALPEEN OF TIM DOWNS, AT DUNMORE.

helped to erase communities from the record. The dead or departed inhabitants of villages that no longer stand had named their places coherently in Irish, but as Friel's play *Translations* illustrates, English-language versions were already unstable: arbitrary attempts at translation or transliteration.

Describing the miserable habitations of the evicted poor two miles west of Doonbeg, the *ILN* text gives no indication that the person shown building the "Scalpeen of Tim Downs" **[Figure 6]** is a woman, with a child. It carefully distinguishes, however, between this kind of structure and the "Scalp", a "hole dug in the earth, some two or three feet deep":

A Scalpeen is a hole, too, but the roof above it is rather loftier and grander in its dimensions. It is often erected within the walls, when any are left standing, of the unroofed houses, and all that is above the surface is built out of the old materials. It possesses, too, some pieces of furniture, and the Scalpeen is altogether superior to the Scalp (*ILN*, December 15, 1849).

Scailp is a word in Irish generally understood as a hollow under a rock, perhaps enlarged by digging or building, or an improvised structure where animals or people might shelter from rain or hail; "scalpeen" renders a diminutive, or distancing form, *scailpín*. Such shelters, usually for sheep, can still be seen in the west of Ireland, built or dug into field boundaries, and it is not hard to imagine the poorest people adapting the same technique for themselves and their families when they found themselves homeless. *Scailpín* means nothing more technical than "a shelter that is not exactly a *scailp*".

The people who constructed "scalps" and "scalpeens" were using skills developed in better times for temporary stays away from home. Fishermen stranded overnight on islands or remote coastlines knew how to improvise shelters, as did people cutting turf (peat) for fuel on outlying bogs. Hillwalkers in remote parts of Ireland and Scotland sometimes encounter small shelters made by modifying natural features or by building, depending on the terrain: in Scotland they are called "shielings", in Ireland "booley huts" **[Figure 7]**, and a significant body of traditional song remembers them as scenes of courtship and light-hearted play. *Buaile* meant a milking place – usually on upland pasture – where young people drove their families' cattle for the summer months to graze them on late-growing grass and to keep them away from food crops. This was once a worldwide practice, whose technical name (from French) is transhumance (Evans, 34–8 Robinson 336). In 1911 Thomas J. Westropp noted that Mount Callan is "girt by a series of boolies". His note refers to fifteen place names around the hill containing "Boula", "Boolin", and similar forms (58). Mount Callan is only ten miles from the "Scalpeen of Tim Downs at Dunmore" **[Figure 6]**. The woman shown building it had probably learned the skill when she went "booleying".

Figure 7 | Booley Hut, An Bearnán Mór, near Clonmany, County Donegal

INCENTIVES TO FORGET: MOUNTAINY MEN, WATER BABIES, AND THE CIVILIZING PROCESS

When Tommy Maxwell called the man who sold Blacksmiths potatoes to David Thomson in Boyle a "mountainy man", it was not a compliment, though it had a romantic appeal for some. The term originated as a vernacular translation of *fear sléibhe*, "a man from the mountain", but usefully expressed the conflation of remote places, ungainly bodies, and primitive habits that became a staple of popular thinking about Ireland following the publication of Charles Darwin's *On the Origin of Species* in 1859 and the Fenian uprising of 1867. It found its strongest expression in the well-known racist cartoons showing "Paddy" with apelike features, in threatening attitudes (Curtis; Foster 171–94; O'Sullivan, *Tombs* 30–2), but also reached generations of English-speaking children, including many in Ireland, in Rev. Charles Kingsley's *The Water-babies* (1863). Written in response to Darwin, it articulated theories about the degeneration of races that Darwin firmly rejected but which continued to pervade popular culture for decades.

Kingsley spent some weeks in 1860 salmon fishing in the west of Ireland with his friend and recently widowed brother-in-law, the historian James Anthony Froude, before taking up a new appointment as Regius professor of modern history at Cambridge.[16] Many writers have quoted the letter he wrote to his wife on July 4 in horror at seeing what he called "white chimpanzees" – Famine survivors, evidently – "along that hundred miles of horrible country" in Galway and Mayo (*Letters*, 111–12). Three years later, he explained in *The Water-babies* that "the wild Irish" in west Kerry who would not listen to Christian preaching "were changed into gorillas, and gorillas they are until this day" (174–6).[17] When his child protagonists Tom and Ellie look at a picture book about the "Douasyoulikes", whose laziness has caused the same kind of degeneration, they are shocked:

"Why," said Tom, "they are growing no better than savages."
"And look how ugly they are all getting," said Ellie.

The children's helpful fairy guide explains:

"Yes; when people live on poor vegetables instead of roast beef and plum pudding, their jaws grow coarse, like the poor Paddies who eat potatoes." (220)

Sir John Tenniel's cartoons in *Punch* typify what L. P. Curtis calls "The Victorian stereotype of the prognathous and huge-mouthed Irishman" (92) **[Figure 8]**. The oversized mouths and heavy lower jaws attributed to Irish men were intended to emphasize their supposed close kinship with the black races and the recent descent of both groups from apes. Wittingly or unwittingly, they also conveyed anxieties about the political causes and consequences of hunger and about the unintelligible Irish language increasingly heard on the streets of British cities, where sedition might be brewing.

A mountainy man or "Paddy" stands in contrast to the "civilized" citizen who uses forks and handkerchiefs and toothbrushes – and speaks English, or another "modern" metropolitan language (Elias; cf. Tóibín 65). The contempt and unease of the colonizer faced with the unfamiliar hygiene and mysterious language of the colonized was mirrored in the burning shame of those who saw English as their only route out of starvation and poverty, away from the most tenacious of all disadvantages, stigma (Goffman; Bourke, "Legless in London"). Forks to avoid touching food with the hands; handkerchiefs for custody of body fluids; increased control of aggression, sexuality, and language, all spread rapidly throughout Europe from the sixteenth century as part of what Norbert Elias calls "the civilizing process": a response to the centralizing of state power and the increasing complexity of society. "Civilization" came last to the remotest areas; in nineteenth-century Ireland its most powerful agent was the increasingly prosperous and powerful Catholic Church (Inglis 129–58, *passim*).

Famine, disease, emigration, changes to the property laws after 1829, and the widespread adoption of English wrenched open the gap between those who rode horses and those who walked barefoot in the second half of the nineteenth century, and dismantled communication between them **[Figure 1]**. When blight struck the potatoes, the people hardest hit were the overcrowded Irish-speaking underclass of a mostly rural population, and not all their landlords were Protestant:

Till the Catholics were emancipated, they were all – rich and poor, priests and peasants – united by a common bond; and Protestant landlords beginning evictions on a great scale would have roused against them the whole Catholic nation. It would have been taken up as a religious question, as well as a question of the poor, prior to 1829. Subsequent to that time – with a Whig administration, with all offices open to Catholics – no religious feelings could mingle with the matter: eviction became a pure question of interest; and while the priests look now perhaps, as much to the Government as to their flocks for support, Catholic landlords are not behind Protestant landlords in clearing their estates (*ILN*, December 22, 1849).

Not only Catholic landlords but Catholic neighbors, shopkeepers, and land agents, too, exploited the poor and profited from their distress (Póirtéir, *Famine Echoes* 144, Ó Gráda, *Black '47* 210–12).

Figure 8 | Sir John Tenniel, *Two Forces*

Figure 8 | Sir John Tenniel, *Two Forces* [Detail]

The Famine shifted the social divide definitively. A new, rising, Catholic middle class was literate, spoke English, and wore shoes; its children attended fee-paying boarding schools run by the higher-status religious orders, mostly French in origin.[18] By 1853 half the priests ministering in Ireland had been educated at St. Patrick's College, Maynooth, founded in 1795, with London's blessing, to provide instruction through English, and where the teachers included conservative French clerics, refugees from the 1789 revolution. As in many African American communities, respectability politics prevailed: priests and nuns acquired a "moral monopoly", dictating how to speak, eat, and dress in order to command respect (Inglis 129–58).[19] "Respectable" people denied knowing anything of "bad times" or, indeed, of the Irish language, until revival in the 1890s inspired many young people to learn it anew (Ó Tuathaigh).

By the late nineteenth century, most of the people who spoke Irish and remembered the Famine lived in western counties, far from the large churches built since 1829. They learned their prayers from their grandmothers, not from books, and instead of listening to fire-and-brimstone preachers in new churches, they observed local "pattern" (patron-saint) days outdoors and visited holy wells.[20] Because almost none were literate in Irish, their richest expressions of intellect and imagination were in oral verbal art, of which the NFC preserves a rich and varied sample.

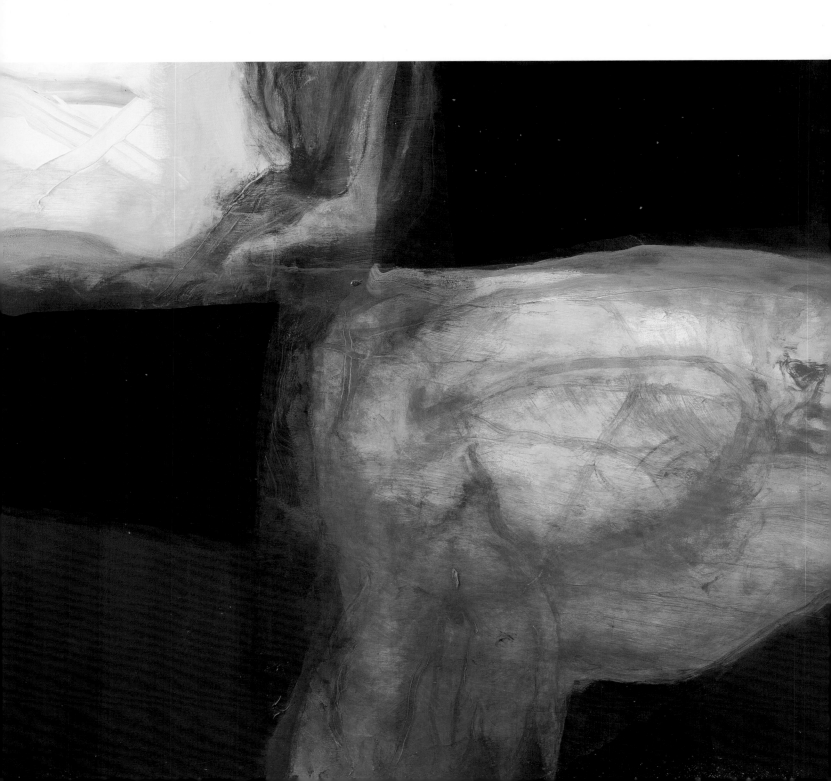

A VERBAL ARTIST: ÉAMON A BÚRC (1866-1942)

Hunger and destitution did not disappear from the western seaboard when the Famine came to an end. Holdings remained small and families large, and as big landowners consolidated farms inland and turned them to grazing, poor people continued to migrate into what became known as the "congested districts". Most young people had no option but to emigrate, but those who stayed lived on in what Pierre Nora calls *milieux de mémoire*: landscapes and social environments saturated with shared associations, where the dead were remembered daily and every natural feature recalled an expression of personality.

Manchester-born Hughie O'Donoghue has been visiting the "living landscape" of north Mayo (Ó Catháin and O'Flanagan) since he was a child. Of his work at Ireland's Great Hunger Museum, where a brooding, contemplating face emerges among hills and fields **[Figure 9]**, he says:

On Our Knees *belongs to a group of paintings which reference Erris in North West Mayo where my mother was born and where I have visited for more than fifty years. It is one of the most remote areas of Ireland and suffered particularly badly during the Famine, but also in successive periods of hunger and hardship extending into the 20th century. "On our knees" was an expression that she used, with its overtones of the humiliating nature of grinding poverty. My paintings often feature figures crouched or sheltering in the landscape and allude to this melancholic memory of past hardships.*[21]

Connemara storyteller Éamon a Búrc was familiar with this kind of hardship. His parents were survivors of the Great Famine, and he himself had vivid memories of the "Little Famine" of the late 1870s, when a series of wet summers and poor harvests reduced the people without shoes once again to rags and hunger, and those who had enough strength rallied to the Land League.

Búrc was in his sixties when IFC collector Liam Mac Coisdeala first met him. An Irish-speaking tailor and small farmer in Aill na Brón, Cill Chiaráin, a place not reached by roads until his lifetime, he had never learned to read or write, and might seem to have lived outside history as a "mountainy man". However, his father had

Figure 9 | Hughie O'Donoghue, *On Our Knees*

been active in the Land War in 1879–80; the family emigrated to Minnesota soon after, and he spent three years of his adolescence there, until at seventeen he lost a leg in a railway accident and they returned home. His parents apprenticed him to a tailor; he managed his disability and made a frugal living, learning to negotiate the rocky local terrain and vaulting dry-stone walls with a crutch tied under his arm. Alert to all around him, articulate and animated, he became much sought after as a storyteller. He was also an accomplished sailor, and when Mac Coisdeala visited him in the 1930s to record stories, Búrc quizzed him about the Ediphone recording technology, and about the latest news from Northern Ireland, Spain, and Abyssinia (now Ethiopia), then at war with Italy (Ó Ceannabháin 16–17). Forty years after his death Seán O'Sullivan of the IFC described Búrc as "possibly the most accomplished narrator of folktales who has lived into our own time" (*Folktales of Ireland* 262).

Folktales, strictly speaking, are long, formulaic stories of the kind that in English begin "Once upon a time", and among which Irish listeners specially appreciated *scéalta gaisce*: stories about heroes and giants. Búrc told many hero-tales for Mac Coisdeala in the 1930s, including one tour de force that ran to thirty thousand words.[22] Another hero-tale, "Céachlann, Mac Rí in Éirinn agus Rí an Deachma" (Céachlann, a King's Son in Ireland, and the Tithe King), which he told vividly over two nights in September 1936, reminds us that almost every household in Connemara owned a cow or two, and that earlier generations had watched their animals starve (Ó Ceannabháin 89–107). In July 1942, months before his death, Búrc told Mac Coisdeala with some reluctance about the appalling conditions he had witnessed as a child in Carna in the 1870s, and recalled precise *seanchas* – oral history – about the Famine from his parents' generation.[23] Reading these painful personal testimonies alongside "Céachlann" makes clear that the story conveys the same memories.

Céachlann leaves home and enters the service of an impoverished king whose lands a giant has usurped. The Tithe King requires each of his champions to spend a month herding his bull and cow, but their condition horrifies the young hero:

... thiomáin sé an bhó agus an tarbh roimhe agus ní raibh ann ach go raibh siad in ann siúl. Ní raibh orthu ach an cnáimh agus an craiceann, agus mac rí in Éirinn ag déanamh an-iontas díobh, go raibh siad in ann siúl chor ar bith. Agus is í an áit ar ordaigh an rí dó iad a chur ansin ... isteach i dtoir chlocha in áit nach raibh seamaide féir dár chruthaigh Dia riamh ag fás ann ... Agus bhí páirceannaí féir ar gach aon taobh de, chomh hard leis an sconsa agus leis an gclaí ins gach uile áit, agus gan aon ghair ag na beithigh bhochta breathnú air (93).

He drove the cow and the bull before him, but they could barely walk. They had nothing on them but skin and bone, and the king of Ireland's son was amazed that they could walk at all. And the place the king ... ordered him to drive them was into a stony wasteland, where not a blade of all the grass God ever created was growing ... And in fields on every side grass was growing as high as the ditch and the wall, but the poor beasts couldn't even look at it.

After showing the young man his duties, the king leaves him:

Ghabh Rí an Deachma abhaile agus d'fhága sé mac rí in Éirinn agus an bhó agus an tarbh ansin. Bhí scrúd agána chroí do na beithígh – an bealach a bhí leo agus gan aon bhlas acu ach ag cuimilt a dteanga de na clocha, gan ní dár chruthaigh Dia le n-ithe ná le n-ól acu (93).

The King of the Tithe went home and left the king of Ireland's son there, with the cow and the bull. His heart was broken for the animals – the condition they were in, and that they were so hungry they were licking the stones, and that among all God ever created there was nothing for them to eat or drink.

The usurping giant here is a landlord figure, with others of his kind nearby, and Búrc explicitly contrasts his lush pastures, protected behind stone walls, with the miserable grazing left to their former owner. The hero breaks down the giant's gate and allows the animals to graze in grass up to their horns till evening. He drives them home, proud of their sleek appearance, and the cow gives twice as much milk that evening as ever before. Next morning, when the giant comes to kill him, he beheads him instead, the animals graze as before, and that night the cow fills every vessel in the house. On the third day he breaks another gate and drives the cow and bull into a new field, where another giant, with three heads, threatens to kill him. He cuts off all three heads, and when he drives the animals home that evening, the cow gives even more milk. He repeats this feat on the fourth day, when he slays a four-headed giant. Land League posters in the 1880s proclaimed, in a belligerent typeface reminiscent of Wild West "wanted" notices, "No Rent! No Landlords [*sic*] Grassland". Listeners who had seen cattle go hungry must have found solace in Éamon a Búrc's fantasy of resistance and redress, as the king's lands are restored and the hero marries his daughter, to live happy and well fed ever after.

VERNACULAR MAGICAL REALISM:
FAIRY LEGEND AS THERAPY

Búrc also excelled in telling belief-legends about the "good people": longer, more-complex examples of the fairy legends Croker published in the 1820s **[Figure 1]**. If disasters like the Famine cause the disarticulation of cultural systems (Ó Gráda, "Famine" 141), then some of these stories, carefully weighing conflicting obligations, demand to be read as creative exercises in repair, "re-membering", and re-articulation (Bourke, *Burning of Bridget Cleary*, "Economic necessity", "Legless in London", "Virtual reality").

Fairy legends are about people, and about strange events that befall them. Storytellers achieve authority and credibility through detailed realism in their telling, but gain a reputation as artists by fitting their ideas and images into a shared framework of supernatural reference (Bourke, "Virtual reality" 10). Their legends map the gray areas of human thought and interaction, which include, as Breandán Mac Suibhne points out, moral dilemmas that arise in catastrophes like the Famine. Identifying someone as a "fairy" puts that person outside humanity. It justifies the savage treatment of changelings in the legends, and may have helped real people to live with dreadful choices. As access to food diminished after the potatoes failed, numerous accounts tell of a brutal triage that could mean feeding the child who had a chance of survival, but not the emaciated, wizened child who probably would not make it.

Humans encounter "the good people", "the wee gentry", or, as storyteller Eddie Lenihan calls them, "the other crowd", on boundaries – of time, space, and social status – or in the Foucauldian heterotopia that is the "fort" – often a circular earthwork – where they are said to live. Usually wild and overgrown, a fort is a place where anything may happen: a sort of black hole in human culture, like Dorothy Cross's vision in *Endarken* (Bourke, *Burning of Bridget Cleary* 47–50; Gibbons 25–6). In vernacular oral tradition, it marks the limits of accountability and the site of legends – fictions that can take over where reality ceases to cope – a haunted landscape where voices may suddenly speak from underfoot.

In September 1938 Éamon a Búrc told a story evidently set in the bleak expanse of hills behind his own house, about a young woman who lost her way and blundered into a fort as darkness fell, to find a crowded room brightly lit and a table laden with food. A woman she has never seen before warns her not to eat for fear of remaining there for ever, and she barely escapes with her life (Ó Ceannabháin 268–71; Bourke, "Language, stories, healing" 307–14). Búrc's telling implies that the girl's misadventure came about because her brother had damaged the roof of a fairy dwelling while cutting heather for bedding. A voice suddenly spoke beneath his feet as he worked on the hillside:

Lá, ghabh duine de na fir óga amach chun cnoic ag baint ualach fraoigh agus nuair a ghabh sé i mbun an fhraoigh dá bhaint bhí aill ann agus bhí fraoch an-bhreá air, agus suas leis i mullach na haille ag baint an fhraoch [sic]. Agus dúirt an rud insan aill: "Céard tá tú a dhéanamh ansin?" (Ó Ceannabháin, 267)

One day, one of the young men went out to the hill to cut a load of heather, and as he began to cut, he spotted a big rock with fine heather growing on top. Up he went, and started to cut it. Then something inside the rock said, "What are you doing there?"

The young man explains what he is about, but the voice warns him to stop, and as he turns for home with what he has cut, he hears a woman's voice behind him: "You're not done yet ... We're not finished with you yet by any means. You've let the rain in on top of us and left us in a terrible state!" (Bourke, "Language, stories, healing" 307).

In 1942, when Búrc told Mac Coisdeala about people he had seen in Carna in the 1870s living in sod huts on wet bog and in shelters thrown up against rocks, he carefully dissociated his own family from those conditions.[24] He did not mention that they had been among a group of over three hundred emigrants from Galway and Mayo whom the Catholic Colonization Bureau of St. Paul sponsored to travel to Minnesota in June 1880 (Shannon 157–71, *passim*; *Graceville*; Connelly). When their train halted in Chicago on its way west from Boston, the local St. Patrick's Society met the travelers at the rail depot with a hot meal and fresh clothing. Prominent Chicago citizen William J. Onahan, the society's secretary, was shocked when he saw them: "The famine was visible in their pinched and emaciated faces, and in the shriveled limbs – they could scarcely be called legs and arms – of the children. Their features were quaint, and the entire company was squalid and wretched. It was a painful revelation to all who witnessed it" (qtd. in Shannon 157–8).

The coast around Carna and Cill Chiaráin saw new settlers arrive throughout the nineteenth century, following evictions inland, with results that were visible in the bodies of the 1880 migrants. Twenty years later, Dr. Charles R. Browne told the Royal Irish Academy that the poorest kind of house in the area was

dug out of the sandhills and lined with walls of dry stone; the roof is low with scarcely any pitch, and the walls rise above it to the height of two or three feet to prevent the strong gales of autumn and winter from blowing the thatch away. There is no window, a space a foot or so in height being left at the top of the door to admit light ... These houses are of small size, about 10 feet by 8 feet, and consist of only one room (524).

A house in a sandhill was marginally more habitable than one dug out of a bog, and would have done duty for longer, but it is clear that Búrc's legend describes a "scalp". The arrival of destitute or seriously ill newcomers into an area whose people were barely subsisting put enormous pressure on a moral economy of cooperation and mutual aid, forcing impossible choices. Thousands of these oral belief-legends concern strangers who lurk on the edges of a community and make demands, exacting revenge when refused, or rewarding those who help them. Storytellers identify the strangers obliquely, in terms that mark them as fundamentally different from "us". They do not describe them as starving refugees; instead, by polarizing revenge and reward, they leave the arena of ambivalence and choice, and its attendant emotional conflict, implicit. This mastery of ambiguity is part of their own intellectual property and social capital, and their gift to listeners.

Unlike folktales, with their formulaic language and many repetitions, legends are realistic; stitched closely into local landscape, they name people and places, and claim to be true (Bourke, "Virtual reality" 7–9, *passim*). Medieval Irish literature offers episodes like those in fairy legends (Ó Cathasaigh; Ó Coileáin), as do other oral traditions across northern Europe, and it is impossible to estimate their currency in Ireland before the nineteenth century. Judging by their proliferation in print then and since, however, and by their continued currency in our own time (Lenihan), huge numbers of fairy legends were told all over Ireland, in both Irish and English, as society attempted to recover from starvation and emigration. The Literary Revival of the late nineteenth century revitalized the collecting, editing, and analysis begun by Croker (Kennedy, Curtin, Hyde, Wilde, Yeats). Editors invariably presented the stories' human protagonists as "other", however, whereas for vernacular tellers and their listeners they were people like themselves and their neighbors.[25]

Storytellers and listeners versed in oral fairy legend had access to a paradigm outside reality with which to think or speak about horrific memories. Defensive disassociation in abused children and the magical realism that emerges in art and literature during violent social upheaval separate the overwhelmingly incomprehensible from the mundane and necessary, yet accommodate both in a single narrative. When unseen forces like "blight", "Poor Law", and "Westminster" destroyed subsistence crops and homes, opened soup kitchens and then closed them arbitrarily, legends like these allowed traumatized people to express nightmare horrors along with fantasies of plenty. Stories about babies taken away and replaced with changelings carry memories of real children whose appearance changed as they starved, making them look "quaint" or "wrinkled with care, so that they appeared like aged persons" (*ILN*, December 29, 1849).

Another of Búrc's legends throws light on an alarming change of register that Colm Tóibín noticed in one response to the IFC Famine questionnaire, which moves from practical detail to coffins seen in the air:

Some of them were wrapped in a sheet and buried. At times a large number of dead bodies were placed in a grave together. No one wished to go near the bodies lest they themselves should take the fever. In some of the districts which had escaped the ravages of the fever, coffins were seen floating through the air (qtd. in Mac Suibhne).

Tóibín observes how, "when people talked about the famine, superstition and Gothic fantasy were always close to hand." Anglo-Irish Gothic writers knew well the decaying, isolated buildings that had recently been landlords' stately homes, but they were also considerably indebted to the dark end of the fairy-legend spectrum. Most of them could recall spine-chilling stories of fairies and the *bean sí*/banshee, which the young Catholic women who were their childhood nursemaids had often told to frighten them.

Like nursemaids in Big Houses, the questionnaire respondent Tóibín quotes must have been familiar with the tropes of oral storytelling. In the passage above, he or she may be recording that even in places that escaped the Famine's worst effects, storytellers and their listeners could not but attempt to comprehend them. "Midnight Funeral from America" is the title Seán O'Sullivan has given to his translation of a legend Éamon a Búrc told in 1938 about a funeral that traveled through the air to Connemara at night (*Legends from Ireland* 64-6; cf. Bourke, "Virtual reality" 11–13). In a more recent story from County Clare, a man crippled after firing a shot into a fort is said to have seen four men carrying a coffin toward him through the wall of the old stone-built workhouse at Tulla (Lenihan 138–45).

CONCLUSION: THE VILLAGE IS DEAD: LONG LIVE THE VILLAGE!

Some of the villages whose inhabitants left, or where houses were unroofed and "tumbled", often with the dead inside, are pasture now, or golf courses, but others are models of resilience. The people who stayed in communities west of the Shannon retained and developed portfolios of skills, as modern workers are advised to do. Combining small farming with inshore fishing or public service, seasonal migration, casual work, and sophisticated traditions of music and storytelling, they remained in their beautiful landscapes, helped by emigrant relatives and by small government subventions, until tourism and small industry lifted living standards in the 1960s. West Clare became a magnet for traditional musicians worldwide, thanks to artists like piper Willie Clancy from Miltown Malbay, Micho, Gussie, and Pakie Russell of Doolin, and fiddle player and storyteller Martin "Junior" Crehan. Born and raised in Ballymackea Beg, in the formerly devastated parish of Kilmurry Ibrickane, Crehan (1908–98) traveled widely with his music and received many honors, but an otherwise humorous story he told about Kilrush workhouse in 1990 included a bitter recollection of the way husbands and wives, parents and children had been separated there (Munnelly 128–39). Two years later he told his own Famine story on radio: "My grandmother was born in a field in the bad times, Bridget Barry from Inagh. They were evicted, and I suppose the poor mother was frightened, and she had the baby at the corner of a wall in the field. I often heard them saying that" (RTÉ Radio 1, qtd. in Ó Gráda, *Ireland Before and After the Famine* 98).

In 2013 the Loop Head Peninsula in County Clare was voted "Best Place to Holiday in Ireland" in an *Irish Times* competition. Moveen, Tullig, Carrigaholt, Doonaha, Querrin, and Clarefield, scenes of such devastation in 1849 (*ILN*, December 15, 1849) **[Figure 10]**, are all on that peninsula. The judges selected it for its stunning scenery and variety of things to do, and for the community's ongoing commitment to responsible tourism fostering environmental integrity, social justice, and economic development. In May the same year, Loop Head's gateway town, Kilrush, center of the former Poor Law Union, hosted the annual National Famine Commemoration. Ten days of lectures, walks, tours, re-enactments, theater, music, exhibitions, and local commemoration ceremonies included the launch of Matthew Lynch's book about mass evictions in the area, and the unveiling of a bilingual plaque "In Memory of Fr. T. Moloney and the Poor of Kilmurry Ibrickan" on the wall of the ruined church there. No charge was made for any event in Kilrush in 2013, but the organizers collected donations for famine charities.

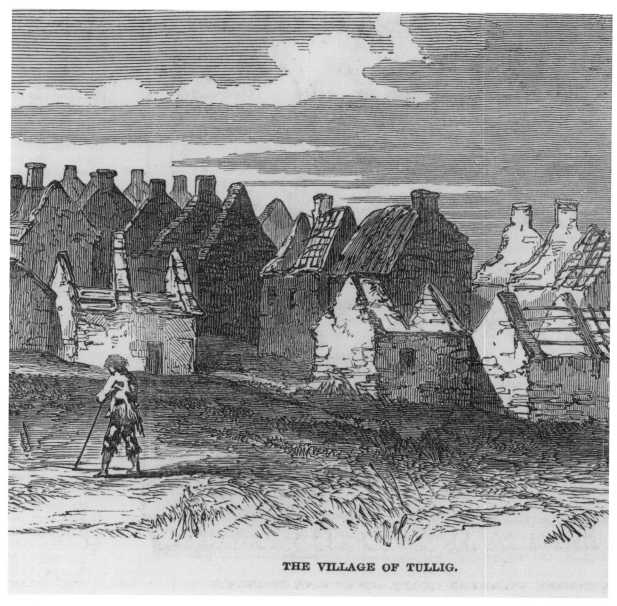

THE VILLAGE OF TULLIG.

Figure 10 | "The Village of Tullig" (*Illustrated London News*, December 15, 1849) [Detail]

ENDNOTES

Abbreviation

NFC   National Folklore Collection, University College, Dublin

[1] The term easily falls together with the similar-sounding *sitheadh gaoithe*, a gust or whirlwind.

[2] I thank Niamh O'Sullivan, curator of Ireland's Great Hunger Museum, for information on Macdonald's background and for valuable discussions. Numerous editions of Croker's book appeared, and the Grimm brothers translated the first of his three volumes as *Irische Elfenmärchen* within a year of publication (Leipzig: Friedrich Fleischer, 1826).

[3] Reflecting a tradition that the fairies have no women of their own, legends reinforce social restrictions on women and children, and warn of physical and social dangers in remote places, especially after dark.

[4] Cormac Ó Gráda, *Ireland Before and After the Famine*, 98–101, 145 n. 8, draws attention to the "sanitized and apologetic approach to the Famine" among Irish-based historians, contrasting it with work by Joel Mokyr, James S. Donnelly, and Timothy O'Neill in the US, and notes that a "leading Dublin academic" derided Robert Kee's 1980 television documentary *Famine* as "lending succor to terrorism" (100).

[5] Avril Doyle, Oireachtas debate, June 21, 1995, http://oireachtasdebates.oireachtas.ie/debates%20authoring/DebatesWebPack.nsf/takes/dail1995062100008?opendocument (accessed February 4, 2015).

[6] Dr. James Choiseul, head of Agricultural Laboratories at the Irish Department of Agriculture, Food and the Marine, personal communication to the author, October 28, 2015.

[7] Irish Famine Pots, www.irishfaminepots.com (accessed February 25, 2015).

[8] The local spelling is Leghowney, but here and throughout I use the spellings listed in the Placenames Database of Ireland (www.logainm.ie). The same spellings appear in the Ordnance Survey's Discovery Series maps.

[9] NFC, Schools' Manuscript Collection, 1037: 113e.

[10] Originally set up for five years (Briody 132), the Irish Folklore Commission was succeeded in 1971 by the Department of Irish Folklore at University College, Dublin. For a detailed history of the Irish Folklore Commission's beginnings, see Briody.

[11] www.duchas.ie.

[12] *Famine Echoes* (1995) coincided with the RTÉ Radio 1 series of the same name; *Glórtha ón Ghorta* (1996) accompanied the Irish-language series on Raidió na Gaeltachta. The Irish Folklore Commission distributed a centennial questionnaire on the Great Irish Famine in 1945; about half of Póirtéir's English-language material is from the thousands of pages submitted in response by volunteers, while most of the remainder comes from full-time collectors; he did not draw from the Schools' Manuscript Collection (Póirtéir, *Famine Echoes* 13–19).

[13] Ó Gráda, *Black '47*, 211–12 also quotes from Ned Buckley's account.

[14] Letter to the *Clare Journal*, February 1, 1847, quoted by Matthew Lynch and Austin Hobbs, Irish Identity, http://www.irishidentity.com/stories/molony.htm (accessed February 25, 2015).

[15] Probably William Monsell, Liberal MP for Limerick, later Lord Emly.

[16] Froude later wrote the two-volume polemic *The English in Ireland in the Eighteenth Century* (London: Longmans, Green & County, 1872).

[17] References in the same passage to "St Brandan" (Brendan), to the "Blasquets" (Blasket Islands), and to a wild saxifrage, "the London-pride which covers the Kerry mountains", suggest that Kingsley was familiar with the Dingle Peninsula and its flora.

[18] By 1900 there were 368 convents in Ireland, as against twelve in 1800. Nuns, mostly drawn from the Catholic middle class, far outnumbered priests and brothers. See Clear, *Nuns in Nineteenth-century Ireland* and "Re-emergence of nuns and convents".

[19] For the *bonne tenue* taught in convents, and contrasts between vernacular spirituality and that of convent schools, see Carbery, 94–106, 134–41, and MacCurtain, 233–63.

[20] The first Redemptorists (Congregation of the Most Holy Redeemer) mission in Ireland was preached in St. John's Cathedral, Limerick in 1851.

[21] Anon, *"On Our Knees"*, Ireland's Great Hunger Museum website, http://ighm.com/ on-our-knees (accessed November 24, 2015).

[22] Éamon a Búrc, *Eochair, Mac Rí in Éirinn/Eochair, a King's Son in Ireland*, ed. and trans. Kevin O'Nolan (Dublin: Comhairle Bhéaloideas Éireann, 1982).

[23] Mac Coisdeala's transcription is in NFC 850, "Seanchas faoi Charna" [Oral history about Carna] 290–3, and "Seanchas faoin Drochshaol" [Oral history about the bad times], 300–6.

[24] NFC 850, "Seanchas faoi Charna", 292–3.

[25] The Folklore Society of Ireland and its journal *Béaloideas*, both founded in 1927, brought new standards of scholarship to the study of Irish oral traditions. The number of related books increased after universities began to teach the subject (e.g. Ó hEochaidh et al., Rieti, Narváez).

WORKS CITED

Aalen, F. H. A., Kevin Whelan, and Matthew Stout, eds. *Atlas of the Irish Rural Landscape.* Cork: Cork University Press, 1997.

Beiner, Guy. "The decline and rebirth of 'folk memory': remembering 'the year of the French' in the late twentieth century." *Éire-Ireland* 38.3–4 (2003): 7–32.

---. *Remembering the Year of the French: Irish Folk History and Social Memory.* Madison: University of Wisconsin Press, 2007.

Bourke, Angela. *The Burning of Bridget Cleary: A True Story.* London: Pimlico, 1999; New York: Viking, 2000.

---. "Economic necessity and escapist fantasy in Éamon a Búrc's sea-stories". *Islanders and Water-dwellers.* Patricia Lysaght, Séamas Ó Catháin and Dáithí Ó hOgáin, eds. Dublin: DBA, 1999. 19–35.

---. "Language, stories, healing". *Gender and Sexuality in Modern Ireland.* Anthony Bradley and Maryann Valiulis, eds. Boston, MA: University of Massachusetts Press, 1997. 299–314.

---. "Legless in London: Pádraic Ó Conaire and Éamon a Búrc". *Éire-Ireland* 38.3–4 (2003): 54–67.

---. "The virtual reality of Irish fairy legend". *Éire-Ireland* 31.1–2 (1996): 7–25. Repr. in *Theorizing Ireland.* Claire Connolly, ed. London and New York: Palgrave Macmillan, 2003. 27–40.

---, Siobhán Kilfeather, Maria Luddy, Margaret MacCurtain, Gerardine Meaney, Máirín Ní Dhonnchadha, Mary O'Dowd, and Clair Wills, eds. *The Field Day Anthology of Irish Writing, Volumes IV & V: Irish Women's Writing and Traditions.* Cork: Cork University Press, 2002.

Brighton, Stephen A. "To begin again elsewhere: archaeology and the Irish diaspora". *Unearthing Hidden Ireland: Historical Archaeology at Ballykilcline, County Roscommon.* Charles J. Orser Jr, ed. Dublin: Wordwell, 2006. 206–16.

Briody, Mícheál. *The Irish Folklore Commission, 1935–1970: History, Ideology, Methodology.* Studia Fennica Folkloristika 17. Helsinki: Finnish Literature Society, 2007.

Browne, Charles R. "The ethnography of Carna and Mweenish". *Proceedings of the Royal Irish Academy* VI (1900–02): 503–34.

Búrc, Éamon a. *Eochair, Mac Rí in Éirinn/Eochair, a King's Son in Ireland.* Kevin O'Nolan, ed. and trans. Dublin: Comhairle Bhéaloideas Éireann, 1982.

Carbery, Mary. *The Farm by Lough Gur.* 1937. Cork and Dublin: Mercier, 1973.

Clear, Caitríona. *Nuns in Nineteenth-century Ireland.* Dublin: Gill and Macmillan, 1987.

---, ed. "The re-emergence of nuns and convents, 1800–1962". In Bourke et al. *Field Day Anthology of Irish Writing, Volumes IV & V*: 517–36.

Connelly, Bridget. *Forgetting Ireland: Uncovering a Family's Secret History.* St. Paul, MN: Borealis, 2003.

Croker, Thomas Crofton. *Fairy Legends and Traditions of the South of Ireland.* 3 vols. London: John Murray, 1825–28.

Curtin, Jeremiah. *Irish Tales of the Fairies and the Ghost World.* [*Tales of the Fairies and of the Ghost World, Collected from Oral Tradition in South-west Munster*]. 1895. Mineola, NY: Dover, 2000.

Curtis, Jr, Lewis Perry. *Apes and Angels: The Irishman in Victorian Caricature.* 1971. Revised edn. Washington, DC and London: Smithsonian Institution Press, 1997.

Elias, Norbert. *The Civilizing Process: The History of Manners* and *State Formation and Civilization.* 1939. Trans. Edmund Jephcott. Oxford: Blackwell, 1994.

Evans, E. Estyn. *Irish Folk Ways.* London: Routledge and Kegan Paul, 1957.

Foster, R. F. *Paddy and Mr Punch: Connections in Irish and English History.* London: Allen Lane, the Penguin Press, 1993.

Friel, Brian. *Translations.* London and Boston, MA: Faber, 1981.

Gibbons, Luke. *Limits of the Visible: Representing the Great Hunger*. Hamden, CT: Ireland's Great Hunger Museum/Quinnipiac University Press, 2014.

Goffman, Erving. *Stigma: Notes on the Management of Spoiled Identity.* 1963. Harmondsworth: Penguin, 1968.

Graceville: The "Connemaras" in Minnesota (DVD). Researched and narrated by Seosamh Ó Cuaig. Written by Bob Quinn. Cinegael, 1997.

Heaney, Seamus. "The heart of a vanished world". *Guardian.* February 21, 2001.

Hyde, Douglas, ed. and trans. *Beside the Fire: A Collection of Irish Gaelic Folk Stories*. London: David Nutt, 1890. https://archive.org/details/besidefirecollec00hyde (accessed November 25, 2015).

Inglis, Tom. *Moral Monopoly: The Rise and Fall of the Catholic Church in Modern Ireland*. 1987. Dublin: UCD Press, 1998.

Kennedy, Patrick. *Legendary Fictions of the Irish Celts*. 1866. London and New York: Macmillan, 1891.

Kinealy, Christine. *This Great Calamity: The Irish Famine, 1845–52*. Dublin: Gill and Macmillan, 2006 [1994].

---. *Apparitions of Death and Disease: The Great Hunger in Ireland*. Hamden, CT: Ireland's Great Hunger Museum/Quinnipiac University Press, 2014.

Kingsley, Charles. *The Water-babies: A Fairy-tale for a Land Baby*, with illustrations by W. Heath-Robinson. 1863. Boston and New York: Houghton Mifflin, 1915.

---. *Charles Kingsley: His Letters and Memories of His Life*. Vol. 2. Ed. Frances Eliza Kingsley. 1890. London and New York: Macmillan, 1894.

Lenihan, Eddie, with Carolyn Eve Green. *Meeting the Other Crowd: The Fairy Stories of Hidden Ireland*. Dublin: Gill and Macmillan, 2003.

Lynch, Matthew. *The Mass Evictions in Kilrush Poor Law Union During the Great Famine.* Miltown Malbay: Old Kilfarboy Society, 2013.

MacCurtain, Margaret. "Fullness of life: defining female spirituality in twentieth century Ireland". In *Women Surviving: Studies in Irish Women's History in the 19th and 20th Centuries*. Maria Luddy and Cliona Murphy, eds. Dublin: Poolbeg, 1990. 233–63.

Mac Suibhne, Breandán. "A Jig in the poorhouse". *Dublin Review of Books* 32 (April 8, 2013). http://www.drb.ie/essays/a-jig-in-the-poorhouse (accessed March 2, 2015).

Munnelly, Tom. "Junior Crehan of Bonavilla". *Béaloideas* 66 (1998): 59–161.

Narváez, Peter, ed. *The Good People: New Fairylore Essays*. New York: Garland, 1991.

National Folklore Collection. University College, Dublin. Schools' Manuscript Collection, 1037: 113c–113e. http://www.duchas.ie/en/cbes/4428295/4392197 (accessed February 25, 2015).

Nora, Pierre. "Between memory and history: les lieux de mémoire". *Representations* 26. Special issue: Memory and Counter-memory (spring, 1989): 7–24. http://www.jstor.org/stable/2928520 (accessed November 25, 2015).

Ó Cadhain, Máirtín. *The Dirty Dust (Cré na Cille)*. 1949. Trans. Alan Titley. New Haven, CT and London: Yale University Press, 2015.

Ó Catháin, Séamas and Patrick O'Flanagan. *The Living Landscape: Kilgalligan, Erris, County Mayo*. Dublin: Comhairle Bhéaloideas Éireann, 1975.

Ó Cathasaigh, Tomás. "The semantics of *síd*". *Éigse* 17.2 (1978): 137–55.

Ó Ceannabháin, Peadar. *Scéalta*. Ed. Éamon a Búrc. Baile Átha Cliath: An Clóchomhar, 1983.

Ó Coileáin, Seán. "Echtrae Nerai and its analogues". *Celtica* 21 (1990): 155–76.

Ó Giolláin, Diarmuid. *Locating Irish Folklore: Tradition, Modernity, Identity*. Cork: Cork University Press, 2000.

Ó Gráda, Cormac. *Black '47 and Beyond: The Great Irish Famine in History, Economy, and Memory*. Princeton, NJ: Princeton University Press, 1999.

---. "Famine, trauma and memory". *Béaloideas* 69 (2001): 121–43.

---. *Ireland Before and After the Famine*. 1988. 2nd (revised, expanded) edn. Manchester: Manchester University Press, 1993.

Ó hEochaidh, Seán, Máire Mac Néill, and Séamas Ó Catháin. *Síscéalta ó Thír Chonaill/Fairy Legends from Donegal*. Dublin: Comhairle Bhéaloideas Éireann, 1977.

Ó Murchadha, Ciarán. *The Great Famine: Ireland's Agony, 1845–1852*. London: Bloomsbury, 2011.

O'Sullivan, Niamh. *The Tombs of a Departed Race: Illustrations of Ireland's Great Hunger*. Hamden, CT: Ireland's Great Hunger Museum/Quinnipiac University Press, 2014.

---. *In the Lion's Den: Daniel Macdonald, Ireland and Empire*. Hamden, CT: Ireland's Great Hunger Museum/Quinnipiac University Press, 2016.

O'Sullivan, Seán [Seán Ó Súilleabháin], ed. and trans. *Folktales of Ireland*. Chicago, IL: University of Chicago Press; London: Routledge and Kegan Paul, 1966.

---. *Legends from Ireland*. London: Batsford, 1977.

Ó Tuathaigh, Gearóid. *I mBéal an Bháis: The Great Famine and the Language Shift in Nineteenth-century Ireland*. Hamden, CT: Ireland's Great Hunger Museum/Quinnipiac University Press, 2015.

Póirtéir, Cathal. *Famine Echoes*. Dublin: Gill and Macmillan, 1995.

---. *Glórtha ón Ghorta: Béaloideas na Gaeilge agus an Gorta Mór* [*Voices from the Famine: Folklore in Irish and the Great Hunger*]. Baile Átha Cliath: Coiscéim, 1996.

Rieti, Barbara. *Strange Terrain: The Fairy World in Newfoundland*. St. John's, Newfoundland: ISER Books, 1991.

Robinson, Tim. "Connemara, County Galway". In Aalen et al., *Atlas of the Irish Rural Landscape*. 329–44.

Scally, Robert James. *The End of Hidden Ireland: Rebellion, Famine, and Emigration*. New York and London: Oxford University Press, 1995.

Shannon, James P. *Catholic Colonization on the Western Frontier*. New Haven, CT: Yale University Press; London: Oxford University Press, 1957.

Thomson, David. *Woodbrook*. 1974. Harmondsworth: Penguin, 1976.

Tóibín, Colm. *Lady Gregory's Toothbrush*. Dublin: Lilliput, 2002.

Vignoles, Julian. *A Delicate Wildness: The Life and Loves of David Thomson*. Dublin: Lilliput, 2014.

Westropp, Thomas Johnson. *Folklore of Clare: A Folklore Survey of County Clare and County Clare Folk-tales and Myths*. 1910–13. Ennis, County Clare: CLASP, 2000. Reproduced from *Folklore: Transactions of the Folk-lore Society* 21–4, with an introduction by Gearóid Ó Crualaoich.

Whelan, Kevin. "The modern landscape: from plantation to present". In Aalen et al., *Atlas of the Irish Rural Landscape*. 67–103.

Wilde, Lady Francesca "Speranza". *Ancient Legends, Mystic Charms, and Superstitions of Ireland*. Boston, MA: Ticknor, 1887.

Yeats, William Butler. *Fairy and Folk Tales of the Irish Peasantry*. London: Walter Scott, 1888.

IMAGES

Cover
Pádraic Reaney
b. 1952
The Last Visit 1 [Detail]
Oil on Masonite
30 x 24 in (76.2 x 61 cm)
© Pádraic Reaney
Image provided by Ireland's Great
Hunger Museum, Quinnipiac
University

Figure 1
Daniel Macdonald
1820-53
Sídhe Gaoithe/The Fairy Blast
1842
Oil on canvas
35 x 45.3 in (89 x 115 cm)
© National Folklore Collection,
University College, Dublin

Figure 2
Alanna O'Kelly
b. 1955
A Kind of Quietism
1990
Photo text
3 panels 19.7 x 29.5 in
(50 x 74.9 cm); 3 panels
19.7 x 14.6 in (50 x 37.1 cm)
© Alanna O'Kelly, 1990
Image provided by Ireland's Great
Hunger Museum, Quinnipiac
University

Figure 3
Eddie "the Miller" Doherty
standing in a Famine pot,
Buncrana, County Donegal
c. 1960
Photograph by Lily "the Miller"
Doherty
Miller Collection, no. 274

Figure 4
Image of handwritten account
entitled "The Bracan Walls" by
Mary Ann Griffin
Schools' Manuscript Collection,
1037:113c, National Folklore
Collection, University College,
Dublin

Figure 5
"Scalp at Cahuermore"
Illustrated London News
December 29, 1849
Image provided by Ireland's Great
Hunger Museum, Quinnipiac
University

Figure 6
"Scalpeen of Tim Downs, Dunmore"
Illustrated London News
December 22, 1849
Image provided by Ireland's Great
Hunger Museum, Quinnipiac
University

Figure 7
Booley Hut, An Bearnán Mór, near
Clonmany, County Donegal
2011
Photograph by Caroline McGonagle

Figure 8
Sir John Tenniel
1820-1914
Two Forces
1881
Graphite on paper
11 x 7.5 in (27.9 x 19.1 cm)
Image provided by The Metropolitan
Museum of Art

Figure 9
Hughie O'Donoghue
b. 1953
On Our Knees
1996-97
Acrylic on canvas
40 x 60 in (102 x 152 cm)
© Hughie O'Donoghue, 1996-97
Image provided by Ireland's Great
Hunger Museum, Quinnipiac
University

Figure 10
"The Village of Tullig" [Detail]
Illustrated London News
December 15, 1849
Image provided by Ireland's Great
Hunger Museum, Quinnipiac
University

ACKNOWLEDGMENTS

For help of various kinds, and encouragement in the writing of this essay, I am most grateful to Stephanie Bourke, John Cassidy, Marianne Charles, James Choiseul, Fiana Griffin, Michael Hayes, Mary Ann Keeney (née Griffin), Vera Kreilkamp, Mattie Lennon, Niamh O'Sullivan, Ríonach uí Ógáin, Julian Vignoles, and Jonathan Williams.

ABOUT THE AUTHOR

Angela Bourke, professor emeritus of Irish-language studies at University College, Dublin, and a Member of the Royal Irish Academy, writes about Irish cultural history and oral tradition from an interdisciplinary perspective. She has held visiting professorships or fellowships at Harvard University, the University of Notre Dame, the University of Minnesota, Cambridge University, the Bogliasco Foundation, the Princess Grace Irish Library, Monaco, and Waseda University, Tokyo. Her books include *The Burning of Bridget Cleary: A True Story* (1999), and *Maeve Brennan: Homesick at the New Yorker* (2004). With seven distinguished colleagues, she edited the compendious *The Field Day Anthology of Irish Writing, Volumes IV & V: Irish Women's Writing and Traditions* (2002), where she was responsible for the section "Oral Traditions". She lives in Dublin.

IRELAND'S GREAT HUNGER MUSEUM | QUINNIPIAC UNIVERSITY PRESS ©2016

SERIES EDITORS
Niamh O'Sullivan
Grace Brady

IMAGE RESEARCH
Claire Puzarne

DESIGN
Rachel Foley

ACKNOWLEDGMENT
Office of Public Affairs, Quinnipiac University

PUBLISHER
Quinnipiac University Press

PRINTING
GRAPHYCEMS

ISBN 978-0-9978374-0-7

Ireland's Great Hunger Museum
Quinnipiac University

3011 Whitney Avenue
Hamden, CT 06518-1908
203-582-6500

www.ighm.org